My goal is to

Entertain ∎ **Educate** ∎ **Empower**

children by telling them meaningful Stories

while teaching Sign Language!

Mr.C

The Big Sandwich
Fun Foods Story
ASL - American Sign Language Book for Kids and Beginners
Stories and Signs with Mr.C - Book 3

Story Written by Mr.C - Randall Clarkson
Design & Illustrations by Deonna Clarkson

© 2016 by RDCmedia—Randall & Deonna Clarkson

StoriesAndSigns.com

Positive Repetition

is a learning method that rewards your child in a positive way.

- **Read through the story in one sitting.** Note that the words printed in **color** correspond with the characters in the **pictures** above.

- **Go back to the beginning of the book and begin to sign.** Your child will see the signs as an actual part of the story which is now familiar to them.

- **Parents can sign the two signs** shown on each page and have your child copy you. Try not to touch their hands as they first struggle to find the sign themselves. They are exploring how they can manipulate on their own.

- **Note the <u>underlined words</u>.** These are the sign language words which were read and signed earlier in the story.

- **Continue to re-read each book** until all the signs listed in the back are learned. Your child will love re-reading the books and the feeling of mastering the signs more and more.

- **Use these new sign language words** throughout the day, reinforcing them to memory.

The **Positive Repetition** of the sign language words will

engage the memory, entertain the heart & empower your child.

Thank you for giving your child the gift of Sign Language!

The Big Sandwich

BOOK 3 of the **Stories and Signs** Series

by

Mr.C

Randall Clarkson

"At the end of this book,
I have two special gifts just for you!
Be sure and use your hands to
learn the sign words!"

Mr.C

very

Make a "V" with both hands
Put fingertips together
Pull apart

hungry

Make a "C" hand - start up by
throat with thumb + fingers
touching chest - move down

When I get home from school I am very, very tired. I am also very, very thirsty. But, I am mostly very, very hungry!

My stomach is so hungry that it starts talking to me! It squeaks and rumbles and it sounds like it is saying, "FEED ME!"

Are you very hungry when *you* get home from school?

What kind of noises does your stomach make?

eat

With fingers bunched together - Move your hand to and from mouth a couple times

Mom

Make a "5" hand and put your thumb on your chin

One day I could hardly wait to get in my house and eat. I opened the front door and yelled, "Mom, I'm home and I'm <u>very</u> <u>hungry</u>!"

No answer.

"Mom...I'm so <u>hungry</u> I could eat my shoes!!!"

"Mom?"

I took off my coat and my shoes and put them away.

Hmm...there was still no answer.

dog

1. Click or rub together your thumb & pointer fingers
2. Slap your leg two times

stop

Flat hand palm up - other hand flat - let it fall with little finger hitting flat hand below

Just then, I heard the sound of footsteps running down the hallway.

"Rusty! Hey there buddy!"

My dog ran around and through my legs. When he finally stopped, I asked him where <u>Mom</u> was at.

Rusty tilted his head this way and then the other and whined and barked. Woof-Woof!

Too bad I don't know dog talk!

work

Make two fists - Bump your two
wrists together twice

happy

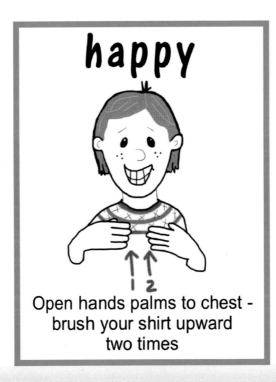

Open hands palms to chest -
brush your shirt upward
two times

Rusty and I went to the kitchen window and there she was out working in the yard.

"Hi Mom! I am sooo hungry... I need something to eat!"

Mom gave me a big smile. I could tell she was happy to see me.

"You can make yourself something to eat..."

I quickly ran and washed my hands. I'm so hungry and happy!

make

Two fists one on top of the other - twist each fist in an opposite half circle

food

Fingers bunched together - tap your fingertips to your lips three times

"Make my own food?!!!" I cried. "Now that sounds like fun!"

Do *you* like to make your own food sometimes? What do *you* like to make?

My stomach began talking even louder and I was getting <u>hungrier</u> by the minute!

(Grrrr...gurgle...eeek...blurb!)

Hmm...what kind of food should I make?

pull

Make two fists, one behind
the other - pull back toward
you like pulling a rope

surprise

Both hands pinched together
beside eyes - quickly move
them out & up into "L" hands

I guess I will just have to look in the refrigerator and see what I can pull out.

"Yum...I think I will have some of this and some of that. I love this and I love that!"

I started pulling things out of the refrigerator and placing them on the counter.

When I stood up and looked, I was surprised by all the pile of <u>food</u> on the counter!

sandwich

Make a "C" hand - insert your other flat hand like holding a sandwich - put to mouth

bread

Hold one hand palm to tummy - the other hand "cuts" the slices of bread

What can I <u>make</u> with all of this <u>food</u>?

"I know! I can <u>make</u> a sandwich!" I said as I <u>pulled</u> out the bread.

I like how bread comes in a plastic bag, already cut into slices. Bread is soft and yummy and goes on the bottom of my sandwich and the top of my sandwich!

I put the bottom slice of bread on my plate...I'm ready to <u>make</u> my sandwich!

peanut butter

Make the letter "P" and spread it on your other open hand that is palm up

jelly

Your pinkie makes a "J" on the other palm-up hand - like jelly on a slice of bread

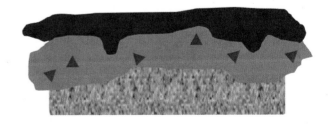

I grabbed the jar of peanut butter and scooped up a big spoonful and plopped it on the <u>bread</u>. Oh no, too much peanut butter! Oh well! I spread it all around.

Next should be jelly because it goes with peanut butter so well. I scooped out a <u>very</u> large scoop and plopped it on top.

Oh no, too much jelly! Oh well! I spread it all around.

Yum...this looks <u>good</u>!

banana

Pointer finger pointing up - other hand "peels" the banana

chop

One hand is flat, palm up - other hand is flat and "chops" the first hand several times

"Let's see...I <u>love</u> fruit and I see a banana on the counter. I'll just put it in my <u>sandwich</u>.

I chopped the banana into slices.

Chop—chop—chop!

I put all of the bananas on top of the <u>jelly</u>, which was on top of the <u>peanut butter</u>, which was on top of the <u>bread</u> that was on my plate!

Yum...this looks good!

apple

Touch your cheek with an "S" hand - twist the knuckle back and forth

orange

Squeeze your fist open and closed two times

If *some* fruit is <u>good</u>, then *more* fruit would be better, right?!
I found a <u>very</u> red apple and <u>chopped</u> it up. I put the apple on top of the <u>banana</u> slices.

I cannot wait to eat!!!

I <u>love</u> oranges...so why not in my <u>sandwich</u>? I peeled the orange and put the slices on top of the apple slices.

I am sooo hungry!

popcorn

Palms inward - pointer fingers
pointing up - fingers + hands
take turns going up + down

hamburger

Clasp both hands palm to
palm - flip hands over and
do it again

My sandwich seems to be a little soggy...I think I need to add something crunchy.

Hmm...how about popcorn? Four handfuls should do it. 1—2—3—4!

I like meat on my sandwich.

Here's a hamburger patty. I think I'll put that right up here on top of the popcorn.

Yikes...how big is it now?

hot dog

One hand cupped like a bun
- the other has two fingers
straight like a hotdog - put

pancake

Bottom hand flat, palm up -
Top flat hand sits on it - then
flip top hand over

What else can I find to put in my very special sandwich?

How about a hot dog wiener and some sausages!

Hey, if I put in sausages, should I also include pancakes?

Yep, two pancakes should be just right.

1—2...right on top!

Does this look yummy to you?

ice cream

Pretend like you're holding
an ice cream cone with your
right hand and licking it

cookie

Bottom hand flat, palm up -
other hand pretends to use a
cookie cutter - back + forth

Now what should I have sweet for dessert?

I think ice cream and a cookie would be just right at the top of my <u>sandwich</u>, don't *you*?

It wouldn't be a <u>sandwich</u> without a piece of <u>bread</u> on the <u>very</u> top...that's perfect!

This <u>sandwich</u> looks <u>very</u> <u>good</u>!

No! This <u>sandwich looks</u> <u>very</u>, <u>very</u> good!!!

napkin

Fingers of one hand pats
each side of mouth as if
wiping it with a napkin

milk

Make a fist - squeeze it 2-3
times like milking a cow

I might need a napkin with such a mighty sandwich, or maybe two napkins! A big glass of milk will wash everything down nicely.

I carried my big sandwich and the glass of milk to the table.

"Oh no...I have messy fingers from building such a mighty sandwich. I'd better go and wash them," I said to myself.

"Goodbye Mr. Sandwich...I'll be right back to eat you up!"

bathroom

Make a "T" letter sign and
shake it back and forth

tummy

Curve the fingers of your hand
- pat your stomach two times

I went down the hallway and around the corner to the bathroom.

I washed my hands and dried them, all the time thinking how <u>good</u> my <u>big</u> <u>sandwich</u> was going to taste!

My mouth was watering and my tummy was growling as I headed back to the table.

Have *you* ever been so <u>hungry</u> that *your* tummy growled?

big (large)

"L" hands - start with touching thumbs and move them outward

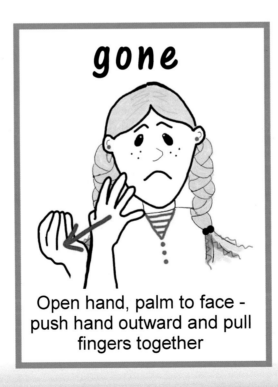

gone

Open hand, palm to face - push hand outward and pull fingers together

I skipped down the hall and around the corner into the kitchen with a big smile on my face.

Finally, I get to <u>eat</u>!

I <u>stopped</u> and stared.

How can this be?

I can't believe my eyes!

My big, beautiful <u>sandwich</u> was gone!

All gone!!!

look

Pointer + middle fingers point
at your eyes - push them
away from your face quickly

no

Pointer and tall fingers on top
Thumb on the bottom
Snap them together

I looked on the plate...
no <u>sandwich</u>.

I looked in the kitchen...
no <u>sandwich</u>.

I looked by the TV...
no <u>sandwich</u>.

Do *you* have any idea where my <u>sandwich</u> might have <u>gone</u>?

Look!

Is that a <u>bread</u> crumb on the floor?

floor

Hands side by side in front of you - pull apart quickly

sitting

Pointer + tall fingers "sit" like legs on your other two straight fingers

I began following little pieces of
<u>food</u> laying on the floor...down the
hall...around the corner.

What did I see sitting there?

Sitting there with a <u>big</u> smile on
his hairy face and licking his lips
was...

"Rusty! Did *you* <u>eat</u> my <u>sandwich</u>?"

"Ruff!" Rusty barked as he wagged
his tail on the floor, looking <u>very</u>
<u>happy</u> with himself.

new

Cup your bottom hand - cup your top hand and scoop it across your bottom hand

love

Criss-cross your arms across your chest

"That was my dinner! You shouldn't eat people food! I don't eat your dog food!"

I groaned as my tummy gurgled. (Grrrr...gurgle...eeek...blurb!)

I went back into the kitchen and started to make a new sandwich.

I love my dog but I think I will put Rusty outside in the yard while I make my new big sandwich!

Can *you* remember what foods I put in my first big sandwich?

bread

peanut butter

jelly

banana

apple

orange

popcorn

hamburger

hotdog

pancake

ice cream

cookie

What goes on the top and the bottom of my <u>sandwich</u>?

Can you use your hands to sign the fun <u>foods</u> I should use?

We did it!

My <u>new</u> <u>big</u> <u>sandwich</u> <u>looks</u> like the first one!

Yummy, yummy in my <u>tummy</u>... it's time to <u>eat</u>!

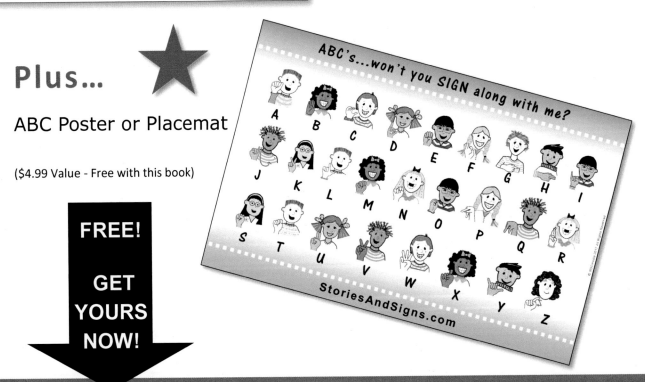

More **Stories and Signs** with Mr.C

★ **The ABC's** — ASL Alphabet Signs

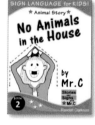

#1 **Out of Gas!** — Transportation Story

#2 **No Animals in the House** — Animals Story

#3 **The Big Sandwich** — Fun Foods Story

#4 **Rainy Day Play** — Indoor & Outdoor Play

#5 **Molly's Puppies** — Days of the Week

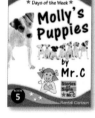

#6 **Best Day Ever!** — Birthday Surprise

#7 **Company is Coming!** — Cleaning My Room

#8 **Haunted Baseball Park** — Being Brave & Smart

Can you Sign these words from the Story?

- ★ very
- ★ hungry
- ★ eat
- ★ Mom
- ★ dog
- ★ stop
- ★ work
- ★ happy
- ★ make
- ★ food
- ★ pull
- ★ surprise
- ★ sandwich
- ★ bread

- ★ peanut butter
- ★ jelly
- ★ banana
- ★ chop
- ★ apple
- ★ orange
- ★ popcorn
- ★ hamburger
- ★ hot dog
- ★ pancake
- ★ ice cream
- ★ cookie
- ★ napkin

- ★ milk
- ★ bathroom
- ★ tummy
- ★ big
- ★ gone
- ★ look
- ★ no
- ★ floor
- ★ sitting
- ★ new
- ★ love

big

We would like to dedicate this book to
our five amazing Grandchildren...

Meadow ♥ Logan ♥ Dani ♥ Austin ♥ Drew

...and the thousands of kids who
have learned sign language words
while laughing & enjoying our stories.

Mr.C   AUTHOR/TEACHER/PAPA
Mrs.C   ILLUSTRATOR/GRAMA

Made in the USA
Monee, IL
27 August 2022

12639512R10031